THE WAYS OF BEING

THE WAYS OF BEING

Volume One

The first of three books of ninety-nine poems all sonnets,
with opining couplets

by

MR. LESLIE HOWARD

Adelaide Books
New York / Lisbon
2021

THE WAYS OF BEING
The first of three books of ninety-nine poems all sonnets,
with opining couplets
By Mr. Leslie Howard

Copyright © by Mr. Leslie Howard

Cover design © 2021 Adelaide Books

First edited by Mr. Gene Paterson Black Ph.D.
Mr. Black was translator and editor of "*The Oriental Renaissance*" 1984
deceased writer and poet in Scott's Bluff Nebraska.

Published by Adelaide Books, New York / Lisbon
adelaidebooks.org

Editor-in-Chief
Stevan V. Nikolic

For any information, please address Adelaide Books
at info@adelaidebooks.org
or write to:
Adelaide Books
244 Fifth Ave. Suite D27
New York, NY, 10001

ISBN: 978-1-955196-77-2

Printed in the United States of America

Dedicated to all, who and what has come before.

Contents

Leslie Howard

Foreword

This WAYS OF BEING is the first one hundred poems (all narrative sonnets) the first volume of a planned series, all in Iambic Pentameter. While epochal in scope each one, each sonnet capable of standing on its own.

But what is the main topic of The Ways of Being? Maybe it is about gods and rituals – Valhalla and Karma? Or maybe it really about evolution – dinosaurs, all those exciting and intriguing ancients. Many referring to creatures – large and small, good and scary, living in the air, the sea and on land from the tropics to the arctic.

Plants, our flora also add to the mix – from rosehips to fairy slippers. Rivers, streams and mountains are not forgotten. Mr. Howard having read in scientific literature, in many disciplines, including the works of Shakespeare.

Is this really a Nature Poem? No, it presents a unified and unique philosophy of existence. As we read along, the momentum builds, and we start to understand what Mr. Howard is revealing. It is a hopeful and powerful world view which is particularly welcome in this time of covid despair. Please read THE WAYS OF BEING. You will be glad that you did.

Ms. Frances Dahlberg Ph.D. Editor of the Anthology, 'WOMEN THE GATHERER' 1981.

Preface

This work, the first of three books of, narrative sonnets, the result of my exploring their craft and trade. After someone of importance, called for a certain issuance, they were my attempt to meet the occasion in some way, although failing at what he and the occasion called for at that time.

Leaving these, the dregs and the dross of that attempt. Albeit revised and somewhat better edited now. Here only because of single positive comment, made by another individual about a piece I placed in a short newsletter. Without which, I would not have considered writing anymore at all.

That and my refusing to give up after being told by a friend, their reading was akin to back pain. Which was exactly what I needed at that time. Having, never written anything of this sort before, after many revisions thought just maybe worth their publishing.

Because I am running out of time. My wanting to complete, what I thought was my last obligation on the earth. To have been more than just another consumer, albeit still ego driven while here. My hope, this book to be of some use to someone someday.

Having my usual doubts now. Always one with the tendency to see flaws and faults in most everything I've seen and done in this world. Much less in everyone else. The incipience that emanates from the arrogance of one's thinking one knows.

Here without any poetic expertise. Much less any real spiritual credentials or merit in that regard. Indeed, my formal education, regarding the above, is one that would preclude anyone from both of those. This book merely a precursor to such. Ill-equipped for both advanced initiates in authentic spiritual disciplines and those who have an ear for refined and poignant poetry.

Furthermore, my desire for the books reading, for any personal gain, precludes any deep spirituality in this author. Since (outside of our biological needs) nearly all of mankind's desires are driven by their ego. The ego, my ego antithetical to deep transformative, spiritual experience. Anathema to the ratifying ecstasies that sometimes occur with those instances, albeit for the most part superfluous.

Thus, to claim any self-chosen transpersonal capacity, in my opinion, is a disqualifying arrogance both on my part and on any author that does so. Much less it being impossible to say or write of an experience, that cannot be expressed in words.

So, no deep spiritual guidance can be found in this author's books as well. Although I do hope the reader might have a look around for some, at some time in their lives. Or that they might become motivated, to have a good look at themselves someday. Yet be for categorical and commercial purposes, its website, somewhat contradicts the statements made above.

These books existing after years of polishing, dithering and escaping from what I should have been doing. Likely to have made my life and that of some others more bearable. Assuming we have a choice in the matter, my choosing their calling, drudgery and escape from the work a day world.

Yet still here, with gratitude toward my editors, and publishers and its forthcoming reviewers, who will and have so generously provided their help and aid, to someone, who they had no idea or information about. Providing their insights, taking a chance on these poems, going out on a limb with their publication.

Grateful also for the blessing of a bit of free time, in which to write, generously provided by all that coalesced in the Universe that enabled it and their launching below.

Introduction

What you're about to read if you purchase a copy, is the first of the three books of poetry (all sonnets) written by a blind man. Figuratively that is. Like the story of three who happened upon an elephant one day, the first saying it was a rope, having grabbed on to its tail. The second holding its trunk, saying it was more like a water hose. The third its leg, claiming it was more like a trunk of a tree. All of them attempting to describe it, each one mistaking the part that they held for the whole.

Like the confabulations of the blindmen above, these poems, but shadows of what they could be. Had more of their subject matter been seen. Mostly contrivances, concoctions one might say, like the contents of our consciousness, that we wake up to every day.

Their notions and themes extracted from some preexisting insights, and adages from a variety of sources, reconfigured into rhyme. To reveal them to some degree. Although here, they sometimes contradict, when not overruling one another.

The source of which, includes the Christian Bible, the Vedas, some Yoga Sutra's, the Masnavi, some Zen Koans, the works of Shakespeare, the Tao Te Ching and some Hassidic thought. Also, some made from the Diwan and Qasida poetry from the Middle East, Central and South Asia. Albeit, from only the surface level of their testaments, their depths left to their adherents.

Others were gleaned from the so-called Empirical Sciences: Physics, Astronomy, Geology, Biology, zoology and those lesser. The social sciences, even some from History and Mythology rendered and processed into various kinds of sonnet poems.

Often saying to myself, clarify their observations; leave their feelings alone. Impart something, of their knowledge, their wisdom. The more common personal, cathartic and emotional poetry seemed at the time, too self-centered, even as it is perhaps impossible (unless transcended) for people, much less this culprit, to work for any great length of time outside the confines of one's ego.

The degree these poems are true to those concepts, ideas and themes of their originators, is of course a variable. Since all ideas and contentions are subject to change and degenerative processes. Due to our and my biases. My and our ubiquitous egocentric perception, when not due to our more basic, ever-present translation and conceptual errors. This work as well guilty of those selection, adoption, and association errors, which cannot help but to be made by their interpreters, when both reading and documenting such works. Our warping, existence, life and our history as it was and said in that time.

Although here, there is some occasional, outright deliberate distortions of some of their ideas and contentions. Sometimes my even agglomerating their ideas, creating something which appears fresh, when not. According to Hume's contention, all new ideas, are but additions to, or combinations of preexisting ones. Thus, by implication, there's little that's original here. What little there is, I attempted to weave within their composition and forms.

Albeit at times, an attempt was made, when composing these poems, to be true (to the extent possible) to the originators of their themes for use in our time. That necessitating, whenever and wherever there might be found an untoward or negative effect from any of my interpretations of their work or if ever that emanating from any one of these poems. Then it is this author who is in error and not the reader, or the publisher, or the originator of the theme who is guilty.

Although sometimes inspiration can supersede that cauldron, that level of the mind. It can glean from the unseen, can gather from celestial libraries, can hear what's on the wind.

Hopefully, there is a trace of that here as well. The better ones fancied, emanating from a source, a meadow, or from some treasury, outside of the human mind. Or from a level, that articulates with the empyrean. Or maybe just from what a psychologist would suggest is only the unconscious mind. In any case, the result of my holding a question in mind until an answer appears, requiring only for it to be put on paper in some way.

These poems about the world's flora and fauna, the sun, the moon, and their shadows on the earth. Somewhat evolutionary in both their aim and arrangement in these books through time. Yet by design, having a lack of completeness in their composition. Their subject matter often untidy and not spelled out in conventional ways. Having an absence of factors, people have come to expect in sonnets. Lacking the usual emotional deliberations during their construction and by design and in their effect on their reader as well.

Yet hopefully, to provoke the reader into some assessment of their own reactions to the sonnets and poems read at that time. Into some self-observation, perhaps even into taking another look, a second look at what else might be had from or found in them.

Perhaps (not emotional or religious) rather some of their own, psychological and or spiritual insights and intuitions regarding their subject matter and what is said in them. Hopefully noting to themselves what happened and what they themselves are capable of. Given both this work's capacity and their readiness at the time.

So not the more traditional kind of poetry designed to have or make one feel. Or the kind promoting or eulogizing something. Rather more to aid, hopefully in one's ability to see clearer and further while here. An unapologetic hybrid of some often notional, narrative, storied sonnets, violating current definitions and forms.

Considered by my editors too didactic, too philosophical, too esoteric as well. Yet the intention, was not to make any one contention, in any given sonnet, more relevant or more important or more advocated than any other. Despite the slant and spin you will notice when you read them here, attempting to express, what cannot be expressed in words.

So, with that, maybe best, first see their reviews and testimonials in their website when its developed. Or, if you like, check out their Blog Where you'll be able to respond to and or criticize them there.

In any case thank you so much for your considering of them. Here is Volume I, meant to read in order, consecutively since many relate it its former one there.

Their purpose: to posit another way to see and approach Eternity while still alive here.

THE WAYS OF BEING

Volume I

To whom we first here pray:

In the name of the fact of existence,
and that of the spirit in its being.
Foremost this prayer to their omnipresence,
their essence and beauty from which we spring.
Their ways of being when a multitude,
the ways of their being, when heard and seen.
To their oneness here with our gratitude,
their ways of being when behind the screen.
For lifting us up, from out of the depths,
to experience another way to be.
When on our treks and if reading our steps,
we might detect one with a master key.
While still on these verdant and mordant shores,
living like sheep, rainbows and dinosaurs.

Ever they're being throughout their existence
one fifth more than the four fourths of their presence.

PURPORT

In need of some guidance while on this sphere,
to be of service in one of their forms,
while on these straight and twisted byways here,
in the ruin and fortune from their storms.
How best to go about our transforming,
and learning the sake for our and their birth?
On this rock, which has us so wondering,
why still alive and why now on the earth?
The length of our life never extended,
past what we must both do and suffer for.
Regardless, what we believe we're doing,
a critical, unavoidable chore.
All that, as if serious about that here,
when most of the time, would rather drink beer.

The one who will fly over the other,
the one more likely to fall and suffer.

JUSTIFICATION

Knowing that first, frail, feckless, faithless prayer,
as bogus as any barker could air.
In this posing, paltry exhortation,
this pompous, padded agglomeration.
Incongruent, a strain to understand,
coerced by Time and Mortality's hand.
Its prosodies and its rhyme so faltered,
you'd think from the demented and doddered.
To whom it's addressed, that too is unclear,
an excuse some say for the ink split here.
When rather let go, quit and retire,
yet, bared from one's own funeral pyre.
When arrears in Fate's debt, in her care and hire,
marred in both her grievous and glorious mire.

Since the essential is that of real worth,
the compass and helm of heaven and earth.

REFLECTION

Yet said all Light, as from a prism, hued,
their distinction, their multiplicity.
Touched and ignited with spirit and soul,
to fulfill their function and destiny.
Latent before their introduction here,
made proficient at drama and story.
Needing both teaching and proximity,
ere they're sighting of Unity's glory.
Ere completing their living and dying,
beneath our numinous, garnering sun.
Upon our effacing, ere our passing
in sync with the intention of the One.
On the behest of the empyrean to love,
reflecting that light both here and above.

The means it said we come about,
the same as that we get wiped out.

EXPLANATION

Ever our seeking an explanation,
some solace, some rest, some point to it all.
When alone in bed, when writhing in dread
a waste of your time in this shopping mall.
Like those blind men, bathing their elephant,
knowing, attending only to their part.
These rhymes and lines, and their subsequent creeds,
all marginal and partial from the start.
Poets mostly scatterbrained and errant,
barely able to formulate their thoughts.
It's why they're always without and babbling,
much less they're able to connect the dots.
Hacking, echoing, pilfering one another,
when only through experience, we'll know the answer.

All what one is able to see,
all what one is able to be.

INTENTION

Here where we conjecture our Gods can hear,
that there's more than just this surface veneer.
Looking down some say from the stars above,
laughing at our prayers for self-serving love.
Aghast at all, what we've done to the earth,
having another intent for its birth.
Where we believe we can actually know,
when our Death will tell us what's truly so.
Never my *dharma*, never with the dough,
having but some sprigs of dry mistletoe.
Ergo the intent is to say goodbye,
to spread out the blame, to indemnify,
the Ways Of Being, if ever they're clear,
as to what could be, behind this mirror.

Such words on paper thought of some value,
in three generations home for mildew.

Mistletoe: A parasitic plant that invades and lives off another, eventually at the expense of its host. Aside from its obvious reference calling for kissing under it, during the festivals of Christmas in the West, some Druid clans had it, that what lies dormant below it, through love will come back alive someday. Also thought to have been aphrodisiac yet poisonous when ingested.

Dharma: for many Hindus, the cosmic order. In the Rig Veda, the supporting and or sustaining aspects of the universe, i.e., their G-od. *Dharma* in Buddhism for many, their teachings, the way, Etc., etc.

6

ASSIGNMENT

Our waking up might be of some value,
for more than just feeding off the menu.
When so easy to break, prone to forsake,
maybe need awake to know what's at stake.
Given the fortune to see and to choose,
we'll either in time, abandon or lose.
Before it's too late, to make our amends,
our having betrayed our lovers and friends.
Before Time and our body's prognoses,
becomes one that's hopeless and pointless.
Might well to wake up and come to a bit,
than remaining here on our lowest wit.
Sleeping under Fortune's incessant fate and sway.
Awake: sculptor, stone and tool all one on the way.

So, what are you creating while on this earth,
if not just inflating your ego and girth?

Although one should be careful here. Since there is a difference between Destiney and the Scheme of Things. Destiny usually thought of as a dynamic from which one cannot escape.

When the Scheme of Things is thought more, how things fall into place, sorted having had some direction, yet not limited to only one possibility or destiny for one and or mankind on the earth.

There being a difference between predestination and determinism> decidedness based on proximate circumstance, yet still open to further influence and change and thus to further possibility.

Especially on the most quantum level, where some believe, especially within a Planck's length any one action in a moment in time opens the possibility, the potential to interact with some other random photon, string, actor or action, resulting in an infinite number of possibilities, existents, dimensions and/or universes present in each and every moment of time. Yet generally felt by people to be contiguous, to have continuity, even a story. In part explaining the need for our and its anthropomorphic explanations.

A Planck length, the scale at which classical ideas about gravity and space-time cease to be valid, and quantum effects dominate. This, the 'quantum of length', the smallest measurement of length, with any Classical Newtonian meaning.

COMPENSATION

Better you're owed for your read of this here,
until you know what to do with your share.
So loaded with didactic conjecture,
better stiffed, than to buy it depicture.
When there's scarcely any great truths in this,
known only post one's apotheosis.
Thinking you might become more practical,
your donkey spurred is far more sensible.
If of any worth, it's striped of its gear,
when not, its mocking and chiding you here.
So, it might even be to your determent,
there's isn't any cheap enlightenment.
What you're more likely to get or receive from all this,
either a fist in the face or a well-deserved kiss.

Our allotment of wisdom for the year,
earned by sheading another falling tear.

Apotheosis defined here: To elevate to a proper and/or to the highest example. The elevation to divine status, or to the quintessence of something.

Also, among the major Mystical Systems, which obtain in this world, the Apotheosis in many of them, it's thought requires the undoing of the ego and its influence on one's being. Once accomplished, those left still functional, having reduced the egos influence, are sometimes able to perceive and experience realities, and or dimensions of existence beyond the ordinary, with the ecstasy and revelations, which tend to, though not always, come with that. Often from they're learning of the real and deepest purpose for their existence on the earth.

The process can be either instantaneous or extended in stages or stations over time. Sometimes, (for those not so well prepared) they're having a series of, "lightning flashes," i.e., insights and intuitions usually too attenuated and incoherent to be significant, and/or of much value.

All that, counter to both our self-serving religions and Western psychotherapy, both seeking to enhance one's status and self-esteem. Likewise, the self-help movements emanating from their doctrines as well. Although sometimes needed since it's said, only competent, sober, un-fleeceable, individuals can succeed at the above.

CONTENT

As in their other sorry sacraments,
what's been scrawled in these droopy documents,
are as much the making of their reader,
as they are the taunting's of this dreamer.
Its rhymes and lines, with not enough edits,
shorn of moral and spiritual credits.
Its content: homage, salvage and bandage,
cabbage for the seekers of advantage.
Wanting from any, the think an author,
something to help them doctor and prosper.
When neither science, nor literature,
culture, magic, therapy or scripture.
More like contrivances made on the way,
like those you'll concoct for yourself today.

Opinionating, confabulating,
barely worthy of the breath they're taking.

RATIONALE

Astonished and bit by their Mystery,
our having to concoct an engineer.
Our needing our Anthropomorphizing,
to account for why we ended up here.
Due to some teleological cause?
Our science chastising that even more.
Ruling our deities>mythologies,
that can't be observed or accounted for.
Teleology and Ontogeny,
held unreconcilable on this tier?
Until both are discerned for what they are,
as the right hand holding the left one here.
Known after our putting, our want for which one aside,
that's if you really want to, here while on this ride.

What you feel and what you see,
all that you can ever be.

Anthropomorphism: The attribution of human like characteristics and/or behavior on an animal, object, entity, even on a God. Often to explain the origin, creation and/or the vicissitudes of phenomenon in existence.

Ontogeny: the origination and development of an organism.

Teleology: the explanation of phenomena in terms of the purpose they serve, rather than the cause by which the arrive.

Mutability: The tendency to change, on its or one's own accord.

MISSION

So were told, 'I loved to be seen and known,'
the point for man and the earth for their home.
Deeming Time and Occurrence to evince,
pattern, form, their energy ever since.
For a knowable manifestation,
created in the Big Bang's explosion?
A home for its brood and their commission,
to carry out their duty and mission.
With a heart and a mind to deal and heal,
needing experience to know what's real.
To keep the momentum of Entropy,
in symmetry with that of Unity.
Needing mortality to focus their energy,
ensuring of our having a sense of urgency.

Where there's a purpose,
it's there to service.

13

VENUE

Be that you're reading this squawk, on this rock.
made round and material by: Whatever.
Its dimensions, laws, and limitations,
agreed upon, somewhat by each other?
Thought independent, external of us,
needing observance for one to know.
Its orbit and roundness, synonymous,
sums, specters, envisioned in the mind's flow.
Current if not more within our being,
as they are and do outside of our mind.
As much our dream, as they are on the scene,
as something one can objectively find.
Manifestation: both within us and out there corporeal,
necessitating one another to do the actual deal.

Both what we are and what we're not,
as much as what was wonted sought.

Specters: a mental representation, ghost

LATENCY

Their Ways of Being in repose up there,
dormant before their delivery here.
Awaiting the time of their occurrence,
in a palpable form of existence.
With their incumbency, while on the earth,
needing attention commencing at birth.
Reason for their season, seen as substance,
whether for worms, or spiritual usance.
Whether when the Big Bang's answered the void,
or were here all along dreamt and employed?
Whether out of some stochastic process,
or for such purpose>the project's success?
Whatever is true, within this mirror,
they're living and dying, all of them here.

Just because we've lost our sight,
doesn't mean there isn't light.

Stochastic: random process, probabilistic, involving a random variable, radiation induced mutation, a desultory happen chanced creation.
Morphology: branch of biology that deals with the forms of living organisms.

CREATION

Since it was out of such, "*Hidden Treasure,*"
within the essence of the "*Lotus Bloom,*"
Prajapati, with his tools and measure,
created the earth and became its moon.
Out of the vacant and soul-less, "*Eyn-Soph*"
where in *the beginning was first, 'The Word.'*
When *Io* glanced, when *Shiva* took her oath,
when the flickering "super strings" occurred.
Within "The Big Bang's affirming, 'I Am,'
to space and duration, Higgs on the lam.
That self-sacrifice of *Visvakarman,*
when before, within Eternity's hand.
All that first downloaded and found within,
the dreams and dramas in women and men.

Every attempt at explanation,
a figment of its real causation.

Almost every culture has some form of religion that attempts to explain both life and existence. Usually within their creation myths. In Islam, G-od said, (in Hadith Qudse), "*I was a Hidden Treasure and I loved, to be known.*" Rendered as well in (Q51:56), in the opening of the *Koran. Visvakarman,* (an east Indian Divinity), was said, to have made order from chaos through sacrifice. *Prajapati,* another South Asian G-od, was said to of willed the universe into being, his becoming thereafter our moon. Also said, in the Vedas, the Universe emanated from a lotus bloom. The *'Eyn-Sof,'* is the infinite primordial pre-existence found in the Jewish Kabbala. *("In the beginning was, 'The Word'")* is found in 'John' in the Christian Bible. *Ex nihilos* and *Io's grants,* are from the Maori creation myths.

Although in some quarters Divinities are considered more visages, names of G-od, aspects of the Unity, attributes of the One, of one God, types, kinds and levels of existence. For the most part, seen from the prospective of an observer, each a limitation if not an insult since reality is always greater than its descriptions.

The *"Big Bang, Super strings* and the *Singularity* obviously concepts from modern Astral Physics and Quantum Mechanics, with their explanations of phenomenon. The *Higgs,* said the posited particle in Particle Physics, which makes for mass, binding the universe together. Said by some, *"The Go-d particle."*

ASSUMPTION

Though not really knowing where we came from,
parroting only what others said done.
Despite our passage through the birth canal,
we need an assumption to tell us how.
Our data but bits and categories,
shards of our concocted realities.
Adroit at keeping our airplanes flying,
flawed at explaining our need for crying.
Though for us, what is true, is all that's due,
all that we're summoned and compelled to do.
Having no choice for it not being done,
it's the way one knows there's another one.
Having the power and the wherewithal,
to make us grateful or to make us fall.

Delineated by the likes of man,
when before in an open fertile land.

LOCATION

When once thought, nebula clouds in array,
folding into mass, molting energy.
Spun round like the moon and set on their way,
new stars in their burgeoning Galaxy.
Held together by Gravity's Master,
the imperative for their igniting.
Whirling around their Galaxy's center,
some of them cooling, some of them racing.
Finding another crashing together,
changing their form and their norm on this tier.
Forging, forming the stuff for another,
needing to expand and Nova some year.
From their wellspring, the Ways of their Being,
honing for their souls to subsist and sing.

Their ontogeny,
for their progeny?

FUNDANENTALS

With seas of writhing, molten minerals,
the earth's essentials, its fundamentals.
Magmas: retching both gasses and fire,
compounding the glitter men admire.
And the stones for knapping their first real tools,
and those for building their primary schools.
Cooling and increasing in density,
every day gaining some capacity.
Came then the moisture, that still bathes the earth,
to allow for life, to love and give birth.
Cooling and settling its smoke and dust,
developing and hardening its crust.
The All-Encompassing ways of all Being,
forging a place where the living can dream?

The soul and spirit, those of that class,
assumed spawned from particles with mass.

PROPAGATION

Where life, it's said, came from the planet Mars,
an affliction sluffed from its meteors?
Say others from even beyond the stars,
brought here by angels and their avatars.
Greening this world's parched and barren land,
subjugate to Evolution's command?
For merely power and domination?
Or here for a purpose, on a mission?
Traveling all that way just to be out?
Or to bring something essential about?
Professed by some but an aberration,
some, "here to bring love into position."
Our past and task, a selected contrivance chosen,
a self-serving constructed, concocted commotion?

Once a photon from Alpha Centauri,
now a sparkle on your daughter's jewelry

PRALUDE

Where first were thought merely their amalgams,
compounding in the seething, melding sea,
adding new forms, extending the limits
of glory and potentiality.
For replication, for transformation,
fitting for the next new member in place.
Selected, nourished, deployed and assigned,
to find their purpose and way in space.
Evolving new forms and ways on the earth,
extending their range and their influence.
Their fate, their duty and their destiny,
another one's fortune and circumstance.
Altering the chemistry in the atmosphere,
sufficient to support a biosphere.

Having prairies and forest with green tree,
said from its alluvial sorcery.

Brownian motion: The random vibration of particles in a fluid
or gas. able to establish polymer strings.

REPLICATION

Since in every moment there's Creation,
birthing another, new replication.
For there to be true cytokinesis,
for the process of photosynthesis.
For those with chromosomes, in proportion,
to make for genetic predilection.
Via their meiosis, their pedigree,
in their form with their ears and eyes to see.
Crying, striving, returning and sighing,
the ways of their being, living and dying.
Having fulfilled their function on the screen,
bearing their treasure within their being.
Where in one moment, all present to see,
in an instant will never again be.

When once young and incompatible
near about halfway habitable.

Since in every moment, this planet's geological structure weathers
down to some extent. Since in every moment the nervous system's
dendrites are in the process of disconnecting and re-connecting in

the brain. Since in every moment all cellular biological structure is newly and continually being created, changed, and destroyed in one way or another. Be in some theoretical Quantum, Particle Physics and String theory, at any given moment of time, there is said only random, desultory energy, potential, waves, motion, particles, strings, flickering like a strobe light on its, or their most elementary level.

Since every time we blink our eyes there is a new and different configuration to see. Since in every moment our consciousness is continually being interrupted and or stimulated to different objects of attention. Since the Reaction Formation in the brain reacts to both internal and external stimuli changing the content of our consciousness both habitually and continuously. Existence itself is like a strobe light dying and remaking itself anew. Be, that Existence and Time are known only in the moment, until the next. All that such that one cannot put one's foot in the same river twice.

Recombination: Gene splicing. RNA, Ribonucleic Acid: essential for coding and decoding lipids, proteins and carbohydrates.

Mitosis: the simplest form of cell division. Meiosis: albeit a reduction, a higher form of cell division in plants and more often animals.

PROLIFERATION

When the air was fit and ready to breathe,
in the era of the Ediacaran,
the seasons readied the soil beneath,
to fund and further Evolution's plan.
The Ways of Being in their earliest spring,
cultivating apples at its Eden.
Needing it green for another being,
for a fling within their arboretum.
Since nothing before had any meaning,
needing another within that garden,
to seek the reason for their existing,
their breath, their suffering, and their burden.
One who can cultivate with rake and hoe,
enough to harvest, to know and bestow.

The all of what brought you,
the all of what kills you.

Ediacaran: The last geological period of the Neoproterozoic Era
proceeding the Cambrian 600 million years ago.

LOVE

Where next to propose was the Crimson Rose,
here with their truth to dispense and disclose.
That symbol of passion, of coming of age,
the triumph of love on another stage.
Told of in tales, in life, in media,
rendered in your encyclopedia.
Embellishing gardens throughout the world,
bringing hope and stock to the imperiled.
Scripture for the wise, attuned for raw eyes,
that red blooming posy, which cries and dies.
Conveying when in a memorial urn
that need of, through fire, we need discern.
What we need suffer to decern and learn,
for the leaves and buds of Spring to return.

Seen it one way, seen in another,
depends on whether we're the other.

CONTINGENCY

Next the invertebrates, in their format,
proportionate within their habitat.
The trilobites and starfish without fins,
the anemones, sponges, the urchins.
Having to crawl about the sea floor,
before on the land, where life could be more.
Morphing into fish in subsistence zones,
having predisposing scales and backbones.
Those sleek, agile, new more mobile adepts,
deep in that cauldron's coordinate depths.
With bodies hardened, all stiff and spiny,
preying on their referents, all so slimy.
The ways of their being within this dream,
bearing the gene for the next new being.

That what's is needed
needing completed.

VERENCE

As are all, still bound to our dawning sea,
that womb of primeval diversity.
Birthing new variants, species and ways
with their needs, duty and their destiny.
With exoskeletons for life on shore,
some even more exacting than before.
Able to survive through cold winter storms,
some who we adore, with those we abhor.
Having their multiple ways of being,
some of them digging, some of them flying,
In their mounds and their hives, in massive swarms,
crawling, infecting, scrubbing and stinging.
Making life itchy, crawly and wary while here,
who we burgle from, poison and scrunch out of fear.

Both clement and cruel to its children,
that cold, aqueous, briny cauldron.

DIVERSITY

Here with the fish in their phylum's parlay,
having the knowledge and science to say:
"We live in oceans of diversity,
we pray and prey for grace and symmetry.
Our wisdom is that of living within,
the waters of adversity we're in.
Our spawning only when it's time to soar,
even when your nets, take us by the score.
Not at all like those, who then close the door,
on whom they believe, will keep them from more.
We've learned how to live and how best to cope,
that acceptance is worth, fifty times hope.
When in such a net, that you cannot spurn,
knowing its function will aid your return.

To learn from the one, kinder and deeper,
need first to open to the provider

The earliest fish, resembling living hagfish, evolved about 550 million years ago. Adaptations that eventually evolved into fish that have a complete vertebral column, jaws, and an endoskeleton made of bones instead of cartilage.

CODIS

When then from the sea and on to the land,
came the amphibians next in the plan.
Digging holes, laying their eggs in the dirt,
where they could develop and reassert.
After bugs and beetles for their success,
darting and slinking when under stress.
Growing, learning, behaving nonetheless,
the latest to express, to effervesce.
Selected by Time to slither and climb,
packing their codis for their next bloodline.
Their presence in the dream just as vital,
their purpose, toting the essential.
Bearing the spark for the coming to be,
per the tendency of Eternity.

Natural Law if it has a flaw,
is when it denies its Paw.

ATTRIBUTE

Even more callous, the Spinosaurus,
the largest of all with that attribute.
Feeding on the hapless Hadrosaurs,
so ravenous and ominous in route.
The paramount predator in their day,
oblivious to their death throes chorus.
Dominance and carnage their play and way,
with that rest in their day in that corpus.
Having the body, aptitude and days,
to move the needle on Proportion's gage.
One of Existence's options and ways,
of turning Time and Evolution's page.
Forever on procession headlong toward fusion,
where in time we will all come together in union.

To each their due, to those who are true,
to what in the world, they're here to pursue.

VIRULENCE

With the snake winding its way on the earth,
loth of both mercy and the chops for mirth.
Ever since creation, repulsed from birth.
The most hypnotic of those of some worth.
Online for the blatant, those at the line,
in need of some virulent serpentine.
With their coils, fangs, and poisonous brine,
to rid the requisite when it's their time.
With no remorse, but for shedding their skin,
thought some pernicious kind of evil Jinn.
Provoking and precluding love and sin.
Yet who bring the vermin population in,
and back into line, one cuddly, noxious,
and disease-ridden rodent at a time.

Everyone with their own commission,
attending to their every mission

CONTRADICTION

The snake both savior and saving slayer,
up from the bowels of the earth's interior.
In accordance with the will of nature,
needing be here, to balance the mixture.
Imparting the gift of contradiction,
grant of precarious contraposition.
Imbuing, priming this show with drama,
spurring our conflicts, spite all their trauma.
Cultivating the theory of Karma,
making for tears and dreams of Valhalla.
They're keeping us aware of consequence,
recalcitrance, hope, love and ascendance.
Both doctor for life and proctor of strife,
making it worth our having a life.

Who wrote the file, about those who are vile,
the one's never bitten by the green reptile.

Valhalla: in Norse mythology: Hall where the God Odin houses
the dead, he deems worthy of dwelling with him.

ENVOY

Next from the endeavored, soared the feathered,
able to sing and pollinate flower.
Living in the trees with the fruits and leaves
utilized by and given some power.
Summoned by the turning of the seasons,
the sincere learning, who and what they're for.
Worthy of their ring of Sibylline keys,
to access and open Destiny's door.
Fit to assemble, to shuffle and deal,
the secrets, the means, the rules in their days.
Able to wheel, to repeal and to heal,
once driven by Knowledge and Wisdom's ways.
The first given use of the Thunder and Lightning,
for all but their ego's self-serving's desiring.

Once such wisdom and our expiration,
dissolves our ego-centric perception.

Sibylline: Oracles, a collection of oracular utterances in Greek
hexameter.

AROUSAL

The Cock was the next in that echelon,
stocked with the specs to rekindle the dawn.
Who you believe, but a blustering bird,
who in the morning, you'd rather not heard.
When oddly experienced at *rapprochement,*
they're knowing its toll, whenever withdrawn.
Having learned its value when in the pit,
essential to know to keep some of it.
Remaining chivalrous, when slashed and sore,
magnanimous, when scarce, when lost and poor.
Still sharing their feed and seed with their hen,
still calling to prayer, those wondering when.
When they're who keep you, from being murdered,
nearing it criminal to have them butchered.

In his own house, he's a sure bet,
in the pit it's Russian roulette.

Rapprochement: French-the establishment and returning to harmonious relationships.

MAMMALS

Then, came the mammals, the mice and camels,
those who you eat and feed to the locals.
With their vocation, finding their station,
on the earth to accomplish their mission.
Hunted and herded until broke and spent,
having to pay for your taxes and rent.
Akin in the order and class of man,
a band and strand in Diversity's plan.
Here to both foil and here to suffer,
used by another, having it better.
Drafted for parables, tales, and proverbs,
to be consumed as if they were potherbs.
Their presence on earth once believed here for man,
when really a part in Eternity's plan.

In the water, in the sky,
and underground by and by.

INFINITY

Next the monkeys with their philosophy's,
touting undetermined realities.
To the chagrin of those who've examined,
who from their science, say it's determined.
In their algorithms, their heuristics,
the latest figures in their statistics.
Their approximations, their testament,
that we're just flesh from the environment?
Had either a key, could actually see,
the gravidness in our reality.
Would likely rescind such testimony,
once learning the task of Infinity.
Forever expanding what can be grown,
forever summoning more to be known.

That what you see and pay attention to,
as large as it will ever get for you.

POWER

Within that cauldron of the wellspring's source,
when it was time for the line of the horse.
An amalgam of strength, beauty and speed,
got poured in the mold of that first grand steed.
For those in need of their winning a purse,
a boon for one, for another a curse.
To bare their naïve sons into battle,
given be someone's vassal and chattel.
Their bravery un-matched, along the way,
patriots galloping into the fray.
In all their glory, those got through the worst,
ending up tethered to their master's hearse.
Unless ridden by Truth and Efficacy first,
well saddled, well advised, double reigned and rehearsed.

All's to be gained trained and reined,
unless you've been foreordained.

FORTUNE

Unless for Fortune, her rain in August,
slaking the drought, in the fields of July,
making ready September's golden harvest,
for those in October ready to buy.
Both boom and a bust for the likes of men,
winching them both down and up from their knees.
Thought a fickle, capricious G-od by them,
here to both disappoint and here to please.
Guiding new remedies, when ill to you,
pestilence, loneliness and wars to fight.
Bringing to people the courage to do,
and lovers together in the moon's light.
Denied by men, when accepting a prize,
prayed to, when needing of her help to rise.

Incomplete without the rest,
in the next you'll find what's best.

FORTUNE

That Goddess of portion, from happenstance,
who fixes, fruits and fates us all by chance?
Who rules by arbitrary circumstance,
if born disabled or able to dance?
Better at explaining, why there's season,
better than astronomy and reason.
Why some infamous, are kept on the earth,
why some innocents are taken at birth.
Why you're here, where you are, reading this now,
when just as well issued form some old sow.
Her horn of plenty, both boon and scary.
fattening the few, starving the many.
All by fortuity, destined by chance,
subject to the one, who's calling the dance.

Once they're made and they're sorted,
rare they are so aborted.

PREDATION

For all the savage, ravaging beings,
foremost are the lions, the first to charge.
Those kith and kin African sovereign queens,
preying on the cloven, free and at large.
On the infirm in their capacity,
in the green fields of the Ungulate line.
Whenever there's plenty, on their bounty,
knowing from their lessons, on who to dine.
Instilling fear and vulnerability,
culling the dawdle of docility.
To make ready all those whose destiny,
is to become the next fatality.
Their tools: their jaws, their teeth, their bite and claws,
serving Fortune and Eternity's' laws.

Confirmation bias,
the root of prejudice

QUARRY

Astir, that impervious herd replied,
"We're still together and still satisfied,
with the laws and ways of Fatalism,
if not the dupe of their narcissism.
That's if their quarry is not at my side,
and not after my self-image inside.
However, so much in our father's rule,
and in our teachings at primary school,
and in heredity in our gene pool,
that all we are, is a self-aware fool.
Fodder to be fired and sacrificed,
gullible, incidental and low priced?
On this rock where the vulnerable pray,
guided by one who wants them to prey.

Who's in control, when on the dole,
in the heat of the desert at the water hole?

CAPASITY

Like a peacock courting his paramour,
like a soldier with stripes strutting for more.
Like a spring flower, feeling such power,
comes from being the brighter in their bower.
Putting gloss in front of capacity,
a bauble compared to one's having a key.
A chasm between one and one's self-lore,
and the reality that lets one score.
One lesson of eleven and twenty more,
Petruchio used to open her door.
And this you must see, in order to be,
if you're to become a branch of the Tree.
However, so much one thinks one's able,
when ground into tea we're medicinal.

Everyone in transformation,
via spurn and cultivation.

Lessons, eleven and then twenty more: The wisdoms that Petruchio
used for Katherine's taming, in Shakespeare's,' Taming of the Shrew.

FATE

Fortune's extinction of the Dodo bird,
a fitting, yet a tragic example.
Like the lesson below told here in word,
whether one's fate, is fixed or flexible.
One with a retort to that mystery,
if attentive, open and capable.
So long confounding us in history,
seeing it as something that's possible.
If able to both read and intuit,
if half fit, fortunate and rational.
If you can retain it and not waste it,
and only use it, when reasonable.
Here in the affair of the fishermen's fever,
for the cutthroat trout in the white-water river:

Explained when the next is done,
followed by another one.

ABILITY

Since the waters from the snowmelt trickle,
and cascade down the mountain's arroyo.
Becoming streams where the fishermen dreams,
of catching them with their skill and guile.
Having both choices and capacities,
judgments, options, and specialties.
Able to assemble and unscramble.
Destiny's inevitabilities?
After all, they went to school and know the rule,
and they can cast a line with a reel and tool.
Telling lies with their artificial flies,
to the gullible however so cruel.
Casting to riffle, eddy lines and pool,
in the laughing streams, calling for the fool.

It takes one more,
to tell the score.

MANDATE

Wading against the flow, until its socks.
one into fallen trees and river rocks.
Flowing before in its glistening charm,
drowning you now, if not doing you harm.
Having lost your perch, with a footing error,
Presumptuousness your nemesis there.
Where once there was freedom, now no choices,
only the squawking and screaming voices,
of all unfit to swim and maneuver,
in that cold, riled, white water river.
Betting that they wouldn't, their cries and calls,
like their prayers for lottery ticket hauls,
bouncing unheard off the canyon 's rock walls,
swept down river and thrusting to its falls.

Information in its amplification
ends in opacity and neutralization.

DONER

In this life of ease and precariousness,
there one, even more fit and dangerous.
In the rivers that serve and divide us
there's the African Hippopotamus.
So, mean, so obtuse and so onerous,
you'd think plagiarized from our consciousness.
Treading the rivers, we all need to cross.
they're being even the crocodile's boss.
Ravaging our hopes, our faith and our means,
our hierarchies, liturgies, and schemes,
our moxie and our virility chops,
our critical personality props.
Undermining our teams, disregarding our memes,
and our conquering and suffering hero dreams.

This one read with the next below,
to help you come and help you go.

MIGHT

When at night it ravages and marauds,
along our rivers where it stomps and plods.
Where shepherds keep, where the innocent sleep,
where the bereaved weep and our children leap.
With his massive loin and his for toed foot,
in the land of man where they won't stay put.
That bruit so recalcitrant, and innocent,
excessively errant and dominant.
Nothing stops those obtuse, impulsive deeds,
insuring their alimentary needs.
With their mashing teeth and crushing jaws,
brought here to polish you of your flaws.
Heedless of your ethics and moral laws,
the one who embodies Humility's cause.

A Bain you feel undeserved by you,
better than what, you think you should do.

ENDEAVOR

Since the albatross was the first to cross,
the expanse of the Pacific Ocean,
riding on warm and uplifting thermals,
barely needing their wings for propulsion.
Gathering way on the capricious sea,
for their swag from their colonization.
Feeding on the sea's surface edibles,
suffice enough for multiplication.
Setting up their jib, and their mid topsail,
indulging in the exhilaration.
Imbibed and giddy on that fine brewed ale,
before they're called for reintegration.
Back to the place, where they had arisen,
with spice and rice from over the ocean.

It takes the next
to know its specs.

COMPASS

Until in the murk, adrift in the fog,
with no direction, no heading to log.
Becalmed in the night, in trepidation,
without a shepherding constellation.
Losing their *esprit*, unable to see
looking askance at the powers that be.
Doubting Mercy, questioning Symmetry
and all that led them on down to the sea.
All what they see, all that geography,
with its plate tectonics and its gravity,
making reef, bay, peninsula and shoal,
soaring rocky shore and magnetic pole.
Coastwise steering them with the wind, the tide,
their compass, their star, their Bark and their guide.

Requiring all three,
to get to the key.

RESCUE

When rescued to dock, to parade and shop,
to consume and assume on *Cere's* shore.
With the means to get whatever they want?
to bring back to their roost, ever some more.
Bedazzled, forgetting it all relied,
on the first intention for all applied.
Via the sun, the wind, the moon and tide,
the sea's waves, its swells, its currents allied.
Saved from pretention and their inquisition,
said by their works, by others their fortune.
Some said, by creed, by prayer, through devotion,
that they survived to stay here in motion.
Forgetting again such cause to applaud,
all with the wherewithal, who they call God.

Sooner or later, we must pay,
for all our luck along the way.

Cere: Roman God of agriculture, grain, crops etc.

RESPONSIBILITY

When then came the Raven, near black as coal,
you might have surmised a species of crow.
Indifferent to doctrine, to faith and myth,
to teleology, anything with,
religion's magical, mystical glow,
realistic in tow, knowing that they go.
Never fawning for a vetting reference,
looking forward to eternal silence.
Contrary to those who pray, when death calls,
fearing falling farther than Mercy's walls.
Not the raven, who merely wants to be,
like a real Maven, having eyes to see.
Better to corral with all of them now,
than to pal with some enshrined single cow.

Baptist, Atheist,
Buddhist, Realist.

Cere: Ancient Roman Goddess of the harvest.

ADMINISTRATION

To run the firm, to save them some money,
a Badger was voted their CEO.
To cut expenses, down to the penny,
from anywhere, but their mistress's toll.
Specifying what our labor is worth,
hiring and firing in their raging rants.
Scammed by their panderers, while on the earth,
cowing to their handlers and sycophants.
In churches posing, at work foreclosing,
the culprit for the absence of cash flow.
Crediting themselves for their succeeding,
when privileged by heritage, class and dough.
Full of bravado, too loud and gung-ho,
our superior, our ego, who says so.

What they need, first is the deed,
to your ranch and to those you feed.

RETRIEVAL

That one who we know, who punched us so low,
who we contend in need of reprisal?
We imagine to be a noxious soul,
a belief that blocks our own revival.
Revealing our hold on insipidness,
introjecting the ways of our rival,
despoiling our efforts at nobleness,
leaving Ascendence locked in the ego.
Its presence restricting our Emergence,
keeping Modesty from its arrival,
worse than religious disobedience,
more vile, more selfish and harmful.
Mankind's dilemma in this world,
one day triumphant, the next impearled.

Where every virtue has its opposite,
our needing of both so as to profit.

ANNUNCIATION

When after the snow, the swallow will show,
and let you know when to sigh in relief.
When it's safe to grow, when best to winnow,
and how to cope with the next new belief.
According to Rossetti and Titian,
the heralds of her Annunciation.
Harbingers of the latest religion,
pitifully turned into bone and doctrine.
That swallows new show, you'd rather not know,
divine until made a faith and belief.
More for the dough, our politics bestow,
deluded that we won't garner some grief.
Those split tailed darters, who once you can hear,
who'll herald the next to endear and fear.

Erecting this couplet,
and the next to know it.

OPENING

Building their homes with their sputum and clay,
abodes of mud, where they worship and lay.
Never courting or extorting for Pounds,
or pestering us with annoying sounds.
Nor do they tarnish, when flying around,
mostly they feed on mosquitoes in town.
Nor do they pinch from your family's table,
and fed their eggs our maidens come able.
Much less scarfing on our crop yields and seeds,
they're tasked to foretell the newest creeds.
And every year, they're so reliable,
the Equinox comes with their arrival.
Opening the *Seal*, with the songs they sing,
inciting the rose to bud in the spring.

The one that opens and sets the scene,
the one who bestows the days of spring.

Seal: In Islam, the Messenger (Mahomed) is said to be the *Seal*,
(the last) of the prophets.

DIVISON

Our needing contrivance to help persuade,
to convince, control and make them afraid.
Our own, so nil of any real helping
having to scourge to keep them tithing.
Blind as to how it makes us the losers
and how it ruins our friends and brothers.
Tainting their motives whenever we can,
creating a bain and stain on our hand.
So gullible to our paladin's spiel,
so convinced our ways and beliefs are real.
The choosing of our-selves knowing what's right,
dumb to how it dims and freezes our light.
Our claiming that the other is ruinous,
the proof our doctrine is twisted and noxious.

As was practiced here,
seen in this mirror.

DESTINY

Albeit, all rivers press for the sea,
liable for so much of what's to be.
Sometimes ample for the crops in the fields,
sometimes they're depriving men of their yields.
In time surmounting our levies with ease,
in their wake, both fortunes and tragedies.
They're making and breaking our hierarchies,
our ceremonies and idolatries.
Drowning our animals, our tangibles,
our ideologies and our scruples.
They're bearing our bones and souls to the sea,
debris and foodstuffs for another's glee.
When then we come to experience and see,
that death is required for life to be.

The sea extends, then it condemns,
where it begins, it also ends.

MIMICRY

With all that crying and emphasizing,
that it all comes from work and assertion?
That what's allocated to the idle,
disparages the pains of exertion?
Alleged by the pundits on the talk shows,
their conjectures, their levers as needed.
Both bate and tools for their accusations,
rationalized, spangled and repeated.
With their prayers and their vituperations,
chastising one another for the poor.
Wallowing in their incriminations,
projecting it on to them even more.
Blind to one another's debt to each other,
each one another's bail-bondsmen and keeper.

Without at least a modicum,
not so gavid of an outcome.

ENTERPRISE

Though the spinning silkworm, said in her turn,
that it's only through effort one can learn.
That the way of the Antinomian,
is one of assumption and opinion.
An alibi for the sedentary,
their duty shirked for others to carry.
When true value comes from working the loom,
weaving apparel from one's own cocoon.
The proctor of one's own resurrection,
responsible for your own ascension.
Value added the Corporation's way,
for the fines and taxes, you need to pay.
Having a say and some spending money,
their measure of merit and mastery.

Some directing
some pandering,

Antinomian, one who believes faith is enough.

SPIN

Come on, the Spider said, "That silkworm's thread,
but cloaks an envious propensity.
To know the essence of the aforesaid,
need pull down those veils of frivolity.
Not only that, in your corporate hat,
you'll just practice insensitivity.
Instead, what it takes, to fix your mistakes,
to reconcile your part in Enmity.
Like those at the mouth of the Prophet's cave,
blinded by Power and Hierarchy.
Authority's strumpet, soldier and slave,
bamboozled by their web's intricacy.
Putting loyalty over amnesty,
so not to see themselves as puppetry.

Implement of enmity,
moving toward humility

A spider once saved Mohammed the Prophet of Islam, by weaving its web over the mouth of a cave, where he had taken refuge. His adversaries' noticing assumed that he couldn't have been in inside, that he would have broken their web getting in. It's causing them to look elsewhere.

JUSTICE

Noted when the house mouse lobbied his King,
who in this case was a fly eating frog.
To have all the felines collect and bring,
restitution to the mice on their slog.
Or have they pay a lethality tax,
for at least a modicum of justice.
After their sinister mouse malleus acts,
of bias, violence and prejudice.
But the mouse wound up incarcerated,
for his own pilfering, the Miller's grain.
That self-chosen Preacher near as wicked,
as any pompous, hominid that vain.
Flitching from their granaries in the fog,
blaming the penurious in the bog.

To get un-hexed
need read the next.

PROPORTION

Since iniquity lives in all of us,
demanding some share of our consciousness.
Including that within the morning dawn,
bringing its serving of misery on.
Thought so glorious, luminous and fair,
until when its storm clouds veer up and flare.
Like a rosa rose with her thorns enclosed,
piercing even the innocent, exposed.
Heart in our hand every day, every night,
feeling our motives to be true and right.
Until we learn that there's no other way,
but to love both the darkness and the day.
Ever sowing in our spirt and soul,
the method and manner we rock and roll.

Conforming to the law,
you think without a flaw.

DATA

Having got to where our algorithms,
it's thought can copycat what we can do.
Their heuristics and usability
almost ready to be able to sue.
So proficient, efficient and astute,
they can light up and can show us the way?
Able to determine a better route,
and an easier way to buy and pay.
That their loops in an association,
in some computer's statistical run,
can see and account for every action,
both in the center and under the sun?
Nonetheless still feckless within their being,
at to what it takes to make sense and meaning.

Where there's some data, one must pay,
with attention to know the way.

DAGs- directed acyclic graphs e.g., "causal loops?"

OPTION

Where on a cold, bronze horse, you'll sit frozen,
your name and fame etched on some brass below.
That's if so far, there's one you've chosen,
loyal to what you imagine you know.
And you'll get a sword form those on the Board,
for being intrepid and capable.
To point at this mirror, for your reward,
so loyal to their playbill and label.
Scorching to the touch in mid summer's sun,
having forswore, having taken that stance.
Cold in winter's wind, without anyone,
having played your part in Enmity's dance.
Receiving only a perfunctory applause,
until when atoned and are reconciled for cause.

There in rigor, through the years idled,
until you're having have reconciled.

ALLIGNMENT

Free to buy and tithe with a credit card,
trained to regard as a good way to pay.
Along with Amazon and some prayers said,
taught capable our having of our way.
In time unused, overgrown in the yard,
no longer, that something to admire.
Busted and rusted no longer wanted,
scolding what our desire was prior.
Our fulfillment, aspiration at best,
for those still after their larges and share.
Until our prayers are for what should be had,
remitting nothing but more fog and air.
Existence, wanting something more from you,
than merely your life and the time you blew.

And until they know, will have to make do,
peddled by the sweet and salt in the brew.

ESCALATION

Like the contending, Clematis ascending,
climbing on those who've ascended prior.
At the expense of all those preceding
begetting the other's note and ire.
Necessitous, single-minded, headstrong,
living off another's pain and labor.
Though the more they do so, the more they long,
for more importance, more wealth, more favor.
Clamoring for the sun, never quite done,
needing foremost to be coddled and nursed.
Accursed by their need to be the first one,
to ensure their thirst is slaked and reversed.
The one in the garden, that three-foot vine,
the last to be mashed and turned into wine.

The one you believe holds you back
best to give them a bit slack.

Clematis: A climbing plant that climbs on others in North America.

CONTEMPLATION

Where, when after those forty days of rains,
there came from a far the gray Wetland Cranes.
Needing relief from their fear and belief,
that compared to death our life is too brief.
Longing for a place to worship and dwell,
asserted within the monastic cell.
Needing to grieve and read from the Bibles,
to buy favor, building their cathedrals.
Where through abstinence, labor and penance,
could bear their dread of eternal silence.
In compliance, in complete reliance,
on obedience, to ease their sentence.
Having looked so deep into the abyss,
there wasn't another way to exist.

Given a place to face oblivion,
where they could atone and pray for heaven.

ENDEVOR

If only they knew, would later pray for,
amnesia if not for oblivion.
Haven, refuge from their pain and anguish,
regardless of they're taking Communion.
Our traumas too tortuous to withstand,
when there's no hope, or reason anymore.
When rescue's only for the deserving,
having had swam too far from the shore.
When the dawn brings nothing but hopelessness,
when our rose water loses its flavor.
When sleep brings grace, assistance and relief,
it becomes our pursuit, our endeavor.
When nothing functions approaching the end,
when nothing will return, abate or mend.

There's hope in the next one
albeit and end run

HELP

What then is the secret, one that obtains?
That can part the waters, assuage our pains.
One that when wanted, can lose our restraints,
one that can deal with our ego's complaints?
Some cloud will tell you; you'll never find one,
that you can partake of, while on your run.
Since all you do is buy and dialogue,
pretending you're not a swathe of the fog.
Feigning that you're doing for another,
when you are the one, who'll have it better.
Unless you're effaced in a sacred star,
unless you've transcended, it's far too far.
Since they're never revealed when and while we still are,
much less when we tell ourselves we're better than parr.

Sycophants for a reward,
never getting on the Board.

RAPTURE

Since they look and count on their religion,
for assurance aiming to get up there.
As doth the Springbok and doth the Human,
to avoid they're being some Leopards fare.
Leaping way up high, as if in the sky
like the ponies on some carousel ride.
Over the glare of their predators' eye,
to land on Mercy's and Clemency's side.
Taking on more airs of pretentiousness,
spurring Fate to mandate another fall.
The cure for their lack of gratuitousness,
a painful landing on the Wailing Wall.
All that desire, leaping in the air,
an avalanche of it, landing on it there.

Looking at it through a glass darkly,
protects your eyes looked at directly.

Icarus: In Greek mythology, Icarus (/ˈɪkərəs/; Ancient Greek: Ἴκαρος
[ǐːkaros]) is the son of the master craftsman Daedalus, the creator of the
Labyrinth. Icarus and his father attempt to escape from Crete by means
of wings that his father constructed from feathers and wax.

RESPECT

Although there is some on earth you might agree,
worthy of some respect, to some degree.
The bee for one, who for queen and for free,
waives ego and credo for Unity.
Along with their will and their need for wealth,
their identity and their carnal self.
As painstaking as any of their peer,
gathering pollen for less than a year.
For their queen, their hive and their coterie,
together to survive in amity.
Preparing their somas in revealment,
with stomas that produce their succulent.
Stinging the greedy, whenever need be,
scumming in ecstasy in *Sati*.

Well on the way and so near to the goal,
the next one will tell you when you will know.

Sati: A rite of loyalty, i.e., in some Sikh and Hindu communities
in India, widows in the past were expected to immolate themselves
on their husband's funeral pyre to demonstrate their fidelity. Bees
also tend to die after stinging.

Also (Sat) in ancient Sanskrit, is the force that emanates (from
the G-od Shiva) becoming the process of creation.

INCENTIVE

Though not quite your preeminent sages,
opting for paradise, for their wages.
Easily rendered inept by the smoker,
caught and bought by the beekeeper's broker.
Barely learning of their keeper's preacher,
less, their minister's embracing teacher.
In ecstasy gathering their honey,
laboring only when warm and sunny.
Before through the pain and all the pages,
the soul's stations, its tasks, states and stages.
Unable to pollenate the austere,
or bring to the ill another good year.
Un like those, who've earned, who've
learned, no longer sprung youth,
that ecstasy's pale, next to love, wedded to truth.

What you intended not so commended,
when it comes from the self-recommended.

ACUMEN

So many purporting to see and know,
like the above and those scheduled below.
Certain of the truth in their assertion,
that they have the true G-od given version.
Of the real, that if tithed and were heeded,
would help them thrive and get what they needed.
Those self-chosen, who say and who suppose,
what's best to believe and best to oppose.
Oblivious such assertions corrupt,
what comes down from heaven and what goes up.
In our hearts and in Wikipedia,
in our temples and in the media.
Those of us who won't learn from the other,
who claim were the ones, who have the answer.

There's some who know and some who won't,
those who tell you are the ones that don't.

CONTACT

'Still fluttering out there on the walk in,
thinking that maybe she's still in the sky?
Sapping her energy, bucking this storm,
'might have to Certify to get her dry.'
No one else out there, waiting around here,
maybe be with her a couple of nights.
Wouldn't survive on the concrete out there,
according to the weather satellites.
Looking cheyney? Maybe delirious,
a blue code, maybe save her, the Crash Cart?
A frequent flyer, said not that serious,
looks way too frail, too old for a jump start.
God, please don't let it be her wedding night!
You need to dictate or postpone her plight!

There's one on every meter of land,
needing a scolding and helping hand.

Certify: in this case putting an involuntary, long-term mental
health and or drug abuse hold and treat on someone for treatment
in psychiatric facility.

Cheyne Stokes: An abnormal pattern of breathing, often when and before dying.

Code Blue: An announcement in a hospital, alerting staff to an existing medical emergency.

Crash cart: Slang for a mobile wheeled cart/chest containing emergency apparatus, equipment and lifesaving medicine for use in an emergency at bed side.

Jump Start: Slang for both electrical cardio-resuscitation and/or cardio conversion.

FEELINGS

So pretentious, self-righteous and maudlin,
brandishing an emotional problem.
One-minute crying, the loss of a doll,
bragging in the next, that we made the call.
Might as well be drunk, on some cheap liquor,
than be someone capable and brighter.
Failing as oft as we are successful.
when declared to be better than able.
Pretending to be sound and together,
indulging in emotional glitter.
With such feeling thought so cogent and high,
anyone can get eating apple pie.
Obstructing of our knowing the answer,
feeling such feelings will take one further.

Like a buffoon you bellow at the moon,
and you wonder why they think you're a loon.

BALANCE

Claiming on earth, that Balance is lacking,
that we're on the verge of catastrophe,
from the ice melting, from the seas rising,
that we'll all fall like Rome did tragically.
That nature's way in one of turpitude,
making and delivering depravity!
Regardless our spiritual latitude,
of our ethics and our morality.
Our bulwarks failing, right in front of us,
our dams and leaves too pale for the gale.
With our tendency to blame and bicker,
who's we should anoint, accost and assail.
An arrogance until aligned with Nature's aim,
when grace and symmetry can return to the game.

The faithless and the faithful,
both simple and foolable.

NECESSATATION

But for two creatures at the Buddha's wake,
refused to morn and lament when he died.
One was the feline, the other the snake,
that cat shedding fur, the snake but its hide.
Their charge and duty bringing misery,
to songbirds, rabbits, to wombats and rats,
without a trace of care and sympathy,
muck mucking them up like bats do gnats.
Neither needing light, so acute at night,
their stillness, quiet and patience allied.
Given both the burden and the green light,
to silence the requisite on the ride.
Here on the earth to make available,
their means to return to the Eternal.

Another reminder,
of that what comes after.

METHOUD

There in life a time when there's no choice but,
to reconsider, who and what we are.
Having to surrender up the image,
we have of our self, for another star.
Until the next calamity bearing,
the case for another disguise to wear.
One that we're able to manage having,
one we can suffer, maintain and bear.
Like the dew on the grass in the morning,
before the dawn and warmth of the day,
each drop glistening, evaporating,
instructing us how to succumb that way.
Conscious, when we're compelled to both ready and go,
their testament teaching us how best to winnow.

Seeming somehow, we'll come to know,
how to come and how best to go.

KNOWING

Destiny thought mighty in her office,
in collusion with Time her word is firm.
A gracious and a most heartless goddess,
despite how much of their merit we earn.
Conferring her blessings and sorrow,
on the deserving and the innocent.
On some today, on some she'll tomorrow,
without design, or prior precedent.
Her storms and thorns letters from heaven,
turning and changing the pages of Time.
Needing kisses whenever they beckon,
regardless how much a blessing or crime.
Our spirit taught to consider and know,
to shoulder our charge, our function and role.

Presence without cognizance,
an absence of existence.

INCARCERATION

Seeing how the red fox crept from his den,
as if had committed some evil sin.
Sniffing and retching, peeing and stretching,
plotting the rip-off of a chicken hen.
Fixing their eyes on the one they're to dine,
without a trace of remorse for that crime.
Adroitly dispensing mortality,
the lives of their progeny on the line.
That alluring, fur bearing specimen,
ever overdosing their medicine.
Quick to flee, home for the flea, fit and free
playing the part of the tragedienne.
Loose and audacious, nuzzling and bold,
caged only by one from their own household.

Like all your saviors, with good behaviors,
as long as from Go-d needing some favors.

CAPASITY

Since everyone knows cats can be nimble,
like bats they're actually more than able.
Careening down with a small brown sparrow,
plop! Right top their folding picnic table.
From some branches above, splashing the peas,
spilling hot barbeque on baby's knees.
Bet you can surmise, how she was displeased,
and how that afflicted that Lilac's bees.
Never again were they ever to go,
even though such a good long time ago.
Blaming each other for that abhorrence,
revealing our contempt and arrogance.
All this offering, something you should know,
anyone can be, the one who says no.

There's some who coo, and some who sue,
for what they want and can't accrue.

MAGIC

So, along the way have you found one yet?
One on who you'd place a big money bet?
One with some acumen, someone who knows,
why we need suffer our tears and our blows?
One that could help us examine and find,
the cause for our famine and troubled mind.
To get it to focus and re-align,
re-set at making Eternity's wine
To fulfil our function , our real mission,
have you found one here, with that commission?
A realistic, bona fide, true mystic,
behind their loan of enigmatic magic?
Will you persist, looking for that one here?
Better off in the foam of Falstaff's beer.

You look for one and find another,
though it's the teacher who pokes the seeker.

Fallstaff: A wily, drunken bombastic character in 4 of Shakespeare's
Plays, having had a commercially sold beer named after him made in
US in St. Louis Missouri.

BALANCE

So strident, needing of our succeeding,
said stronger than our moral compunctions.
Our craving to get and have it our way,
regardless the result of our actions.
Justifying our actual behavior,
omitting the balance in the story.
That we apply to discount another
regardless of how derogatory.
So anxious for our own formulation,
willing to perjure, in our addenda.
Unable to see, none of that's needed,
learning our having the same agenda.
Heard and seen for what we've achieved and are,
denuded without the others one's star.

Angry lions left in a rage,
until they break out from their cage.

SINCERITY

The dreams we have for our life from the start,
planning and plotting our self-serving schemes,
preserved until Fate insist on her part,
convening of her own dreams and regimes.
Having to swallow her despair for a while,
having to suffer, to lose and to morn.
Having to beg for ease from affixation,
lamenting our having even been born.
Begging for respite, when out of hand
groveling for reprieve, relief from her aim.
Without mercy, or any clemency,
when there's no hope, begging out of the frame.
Until made compliant in mind and eye,
mandated to manage until we die.

Sometimes it seems we would rather,
have our way than touch another.

LOYALTY

Where on the Southern Central Asian Steppes,
off of someone's leash, released from their hand.
The Raptor glides, plummets and intercepts,
the Fox and the long-eared Hare on their land.
A boon for both, as long as they gather,
enough to profit from one another.
Each one extending the other one's reach,
for warmth, some pelts and some protein for each.
Their homage based on the installment plan,
content with fresh, morsels of flesh they've ran.
Until failing to feed the other's due,
that's when they'll start their fomenting a Coup.
Deprived of their fur and their bloody swill,
no surprise here, they'll renege on their deal.

Their loyalty based on a royalty,
as long if there isn't a penalty.

EVIL

So said the Weevil, then tell us what's evil,
on the earth, where you think you're so civil!
So eager you are to have it exposed,
so keen you are for the banning its prose!
On the radio against your rival,
adulterating what's in the bible.
Fomenting the wars, you have against it,
miring those you allude as illicit.
With your enemy's partisan penchant,
for blame, for censure, and all their ferment.
Forcing their writing a loyalty troth,
for you to feature another to loath?
All the while thinking that you're above it,
an elevated, spiritual, self-chosen prophet.

*The answer to that villainization,
in the next, lacking illumination.*

PROCEDURE

Since, we warp and distort what others do,
to elevate our own stature and score.
Our needing of clout, having to construe,
desecrating the gold in our own ore.
Our need to concoct and contrive for sway,
mocking their behavior and their glory.
Besmirching our own nature and way,
out of tune with their music and story.
Until made seen through Eternity's eye,
for what we are and what we've brought ashore.
When brought down by the truth and left to lie,
to awaken at humility's door.
Having had taken it right on the chin,
opening our eyes to the truth again.

Another way we misconstrue,
taking credit for someone's do.

RAIN

Those billowing clouds rounding through the sky's,
enabling our meadows and gardens grow.
Yet they do not hear, or have they the eyes,
to know those worthy of their moisture's flow.
Turning them green and leaving them in drought,
unslaked and baked from the absence of rain.
Sometimes sprouting and sometime scouring,
despite our merit, our age and our pain.
Like mercy and tragedy up that high,
whether indifferent or from Karma wrought.
Their falling through the years, despite our tears,
both a blessing and catalyst for rot.
Gracious, ambivalent, loving and mean,
in time they're making our gardens grow green.

Indifferent to your concern,
until it's time to return.

OPTION

Though you won't be finding the Hibiscus,
lackadaisical and lying around.
Their ways of being, more avaricious,
over-growing others, up from the ground.
Where they feel, up higher in the garden,
the sunlight will keep them warm with its rays.
choosing sensation over proportion,
rather than they're letting it guide their ways.
Like those who judge by the gloss on the page,
like all those enamored by chromium.
Who miss the secret wisdom of the age,
passing that diamond for zirconium.
Rather than be led by the Southern Cross,
opting for the dregs, the smoke and the dross.

An affectation,
a missed direction.

PROOF

Our bibles, our prayers, our meditations,
when sold, turning both rancid and sour.
Commercially used and selfishly taught,
sullying what we bake with their flour.
Used to provoke, to arouse emotion,
unleashing overdriven desire.
For clout and money, warmth and honey,
fettering our getting any higher.
To keep us from feeling we're the greedy,
that we're well washed and in good mental health.
Bogusly said to be for the needy,
serving the image, we have of our self.
When meant to bring buds into flower,
for their nectar to be used as dower.

Whether successful whether not
a matter of what one was taught.

SOLITUDE

Though, some in the garden can heal and mend,
those in the winter, when wilted and dry.
Some, with their arts and melodies in tune,
bring splendor and beauty to your eye.
Some with their religion's creed and pardon,
mobilize sympathy and charity.
Yet only the rose, lord of the garden,
can restore both balance and symmetry.
Known by the count of their petals offered,
at the tombs of their sacrosanct saints.
Having endured both lightning and thunder,
able to see and address our constraints.
Key to our essential, spiritual goal,
they're grafting of love on the human soul.

Every time were made to cry,
made a little inner high?

SHOCK

There when she was only seven years old,
a dark brown shadow with its talons cold,
dived on her kitten and took him with ease,
when playing under some cottonwood trees.
So close, she felt an air gust from its wing,
too fast for anyone to intervene.
Bearing him off to his own on a limb,
leaving in the eye, but a streak of him.
A shudder from both, a sock and a gawk!
as if experienced an electric shock.
Her wailing that night the stars of their light,
now's she keeps cats at her place out of spite.
Her first real outrage, grief, and sorrow,
taught that just maybe there's no tomorrow.

Learning to who one belongs,
taught by what were though as wrongs.

WOUND

Where it will feel as if an open wound,
harmed for no reason but having assumed.
And you'll think it unfair, having such pain,
finding your crying and praying in vain.
Your former aims, fallen before your eyes,
knowing them then, as a Faustian prize.
The fate of those, who haven't done battle,
with the part of you, you thought capable.
Oblivious to the need for that task,
compelled to imbibe from Misery's flask.
A gift, having us drop our former state,
the shortest path to a far greater fate.
Since, what once was a veil, becomes a shroud,
until washed away by Misfortune's cloud.

Whether you want to take the time
nature will bring you back online.

Faustian: Alluding to striving for power at the price of spiritual
values.

METHOUD

"Still being gullible, the Virus sighed,
 hanging on begging to stay on the ride?
 To remain on this earth as a person,
 you believe dismissed for no good reason?
 Assuming, never a better solvent.
 when soon with agonies great and constant.
 Complaining you haven't been completed.
 as if were one, whose never been gifted?
 One deserving a love that's enduing?
 One whose penance is bereft and lacking.
 A waste of your breath when it comes to me,
 I'm here to terminate your misery.
 Since I'm the one who with my virulent glans,
 who elevates you into Eternity's hands."

Be in the next poem
the way to get home.

ASSIMILATION

''Here for you, for your reintegration,
for your ultimate assimilation.
Waiting for you with my beckoning arms,
calling for you with my succulent charms.
With my warm honey, on Symmetry's knife,
you think, but a curse, a scourge in your life.
You're, considering me, your enemy,
when pained on your death bed you'll beg for me.
When your misery no longer has use,
when all your pain meds, no longer profuse.
Your anti-virals and antiseptics,
I'll surmount with my gambits and tactics.
Claiming I'm out of tune in the chorus,
when but your virulent, servant Virus.''

The one who's we most not think dear,
the one we need most this year.

PRETENTION

Writing, reading, these couplets and their rhymes,
redundant and bereft of subtlety.
For the most part moot and behind the times,
deficient in both heart and poignancy.
Reviewed by competent critics who know,
their author's lack of beauty and prudence.
Poetically miscast, to tight, too low,
a monument to pretension's presence.
Its couplets and lines and how it all flows,
on behest the ego's wants and request.
Revealing how little, one really knows,
and the distance they are from Wisdom's chest.
These lines lacking both taste and credibility,
this bloke a fly on the face of Eternity.

To open a door
is all what it's for

DISCLOSURE

Despite when alone and lost in a storm,
there's still what lies beyond the horizon.
Able to tell us, what needs to be done,
to renew our previous connection.
If open to clue and what to eschew,
able to rein in our inner detractors.
With enough force, set back on course,
able to learn from our disparagers.
Our needing acquire a nuanced view,
to see what needs, both watered and seeded.
Whispered by that tumult's freezing white spew,
formulated, developed and heeded.
Upon refining and our completing.
given the task to compute our heading.

Within the dew beneath the morning star,
comes the first optic of all what we are.

PASSING

Our journey and our seeking all over,
our needing only to learn how to die.
How to succumb and tolerate its pain,
in our beds, or in the dirt where we lie.
Our existence at best in need of rest,
now that were old, and our life is in doubt.
In the age of this world's pandemics,
impugning and quashing what were about.
Researching our memories for merit,
when not on the drawstrings of another,
for anything that was significant,
that may have been more than just a flutter.
Our having been put and run through a maze,
on stage for another's pursuit and gaze?

Wanting what you think you deserved,
is how you know you won't be served.

RECOGNITION

Our, knowing the seasons both stark and kind,
always somewhere in the back if our mind.
Sometimes darkening the clouds in the sky,
sometimes they're ensuring were all well dined.
With their blessings, disaster and censure,
when love turns into folly and vapor.
Forcing us to both laugh and writhe in pain,
they're schooling of us, the way of Nature.
With their turning and they're changing colors,
sometimes letting us transcend our blunders.
Restoring our hope, that maybe this time,
they'll show us some even greater wonders.
Sometimes helping us, be the first in line,
sometimes they're taking us before our time.

However, many on the shore,
there's always a place for some more.

DOCTRINE

Now since it's time for this volume to end,
ready for you to critique and amend.
Before it's recognized as hokum here,
with its rhymes and lines, that hardly adhere.
Before it decomposes into dust,
considered by many but rot and rust.
Before becoming another pretext,
for Enmity's disciples and prospects.
Wasting and squandering your precious time,
when you could be sloshed on much better wine.
Since what you've made of it, has missed the point,
that our truths and lies are all out of joint.
Since what we see, is hardly ever clear,
if it were, you wouldn't be reading this here.

So now that you've paid for this souvenir?
best lose it in the wind and rain somewhere.

UNITY

Since some have discerned, and others have not,
having taken on, what needed be sought.
Resigned to the blossom they were assigned,
leaving their prior desires behind.
Their self-serving consigned to the margin,
for labor in Eternity's Garden.
Cut and boiled as if a vegetable,
able to pen a sacred parable.
Strewing verity on the descended,
when needing steering toward the Intended.
Given the fuel and the capacity,
to expedite balance and symmetry.
Able to alter the Ways of Being,
permission given when the truth is seen.

Given capacity,
to serve Eternity.

LAST

Ergo, here in the name of Existence,
in ode to the spirit in its being.
We pray to their essence and omniscience,
their Truth and Unity from which we spring.
To the love in their manifestation,
in all that's been established and revealed.
To the truth in their amalgamation,
created, proscribed, imparted and held.
With all the energy that they disperse,
extending the limits of their glory.
In our infinite, timeless universe,
in which we live and act out our story.
Both on this planet and within these ninety-nine,
and in two coming volumes with sonnets that rhyme.

Attention to intention,
maintains your administration.

CONSIGNMENT

FOR THE ONE WHO DESERVES ALL
THE BLESSINGS

About the Author

Mr. Howard, a former garbage worker, dishwasher, ditch digger, factory worker, framing carpenter, truck driver, ski patrolman, Coast Guardsmen, operating room technician, EMT, smuggler, protester, explosive detonator, grifter, process server, prison counselor, mental health evaluator, world traveler, probate court investigator, mountaineer, rock climber, fly fishermen and now a poet to name just a few living in Denver Colorado.

Made in the USA
Middletown, DE
20 February 2022

61457688R00078